40 ▶ DAYS THROUGH

JOHN

LIFE IN HIS NAME

BIBLE STUDY GUIDE | STREAMING VIDEO | 6 SESSIONS

KYLE IDLEMAN

WITH KEVIN AND SHERRY HARNEY

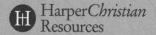

Harper*Christian*
Resources

40 Days Through the Book: John
© 2023 by Kyle Idleman

Requests for information should be addressed to:
HarperChristian Resources, 3900 Sparks Dr. SE, Grand Rapids, Michigan 49546

ISBN 978-0-310-15641-3 (softcover)
ISBN 978-0-310-15642-0 (ebook)

HarperChristian Resources titles may be purchased in bulk for church, business, fundraising, or ministry use. For information, please e-mail ResourceSpecialist@ ChurchSource.com.

Author is represented by the literary agent Don Gates @ THE GATES GROUP, www.thegates-group.com.

First Printing December 2022 / Printed in the United States of America

22 23 24 25 26 LBC 5 4 3 2 1

CONTENTS

HOW TO USE THIS GUIDE

SCOPE AND SEQUENCE

Welcome to the *40 Days Through the Book* study on the Gospel of John! During the course of the next six weeks, you and your fellow group members will embark on an in-depth exploration of the disciple John's message to believers in the Church. During this study, you will learn approximately when he wrote the book, the audience for whom he was writing it, and the background and context in which the book was written. But, more importantly, through the teaching by Kyle Idleman, you will explore the key themes that John relates in the book—and how his teachings apply to you today.

SESSION OUTLINE

The *40 Days Through the Book* study is designed to be experienced both in group settings (such as a Bible study, Sunday school class, or small group gatherings) as well as in your individual study time. Each session begins with an introductory reading and question. You will then watch the video message. (Play the DVD or refer to the instructions on the inside front cover on how to access the sessions at any time through streaming.) An outline has been provided in the guide for you to take notes and gather your reflections as you watch the video. Next, if you are doing this study with a group, you will engage in a time of directed discussion, review the memory verses for the week, and close with a time of prayer. (Note that if your group is larger, you may wish to watch the videos together and then break into smaller groups of four to six people, to ensure that everyone has time to participate in discussions.)

40-DAY JOURNEY

What is unique about this study, and all of the other studies in the *40 Days Through the Book* series, are the daily learning resources that will lead you into a deeper engagement with the text. Each week, you will be given a set of daily readings, with accompanying reflection questions, to help you explore the material that you covered during your group time.

The first day's reading will focus on the key verse to memorize for the week. In the other weekly readings, you will be invited to read a passage from the Gospel of John, reflect on the text, and then respond with some guided journal questions. On the final day, you will review the key verse again and recite it from memory. As you work through the six weeks' worth of material in this section, you will read (and, in some cases, reread) the entire book of John.

Now, you may be wondering why you will be doing this over the course of *forty* days. Certainly, there is nothing special about that number. But there is something biblical about it. In the Bible, the number forty typically designates a time of *testing*. Noah was in the ark for forty days. Moses lived forty years in Egypt and another forty years in the desert before he led God's people. He spent forty days on Mount Sinai receiving God's laws and sent spies, for forty days, to investigate the land of Canaan. Later, God sent the prophet Jonah to warn ancient Nineveh, for forty days, that its destruction would come because of the people's sins.

Even more critically, in the New Testament we read that Jesus spent forty days in the wilderness, fasting and praying. It marked a critical transition point in his ministry—the place where he set about to fulfill the mission that God had intended. During this time Jesus was tested relentlessly by the enemy . . . and prevailed. When he returned to Galilee, he was a different person than the man who had entered into the wilderness forty days before. The same will be true for you as you commit to this forty-day journey through John.

GROUP FACILITATION

If you are doing this study with a group, everyone should have a copy of this study guide. Not only will this help you engage when your group is meeting, but it will also allow you to fully enter into the *40 Days* learning experience. Keep in mind the video, questions, and activities are simply tools to help you engage with the session. The real power and life-transformation will come as you dig into the Scriptures and seek to live out the truths you learn along the way.

Finally, you will need to appoint a leader or facilitator for the group who is responsible for starting the video teaching and for keeping track of time during discussions and activities. Leaders may also read questions aloud and monitor discussions, prompting participants to respond and ensuring that everyone has the opportunity to participate. For more thorough instructions on this role, see the Leader's Guide included at the back of this guide.

INTRODUCTION

JOHN

AUTHOR, DATE, AND LOCATION

During his years of ministry, Jesus spoke to the masses, sent out the Seventy, and called the Twelve, but he also had an inner circle of three disciples: Peter, James, and John. The author of this Gospel is one of them. John, the beloved disciple, was one of the Savior's dearest friends and partners in ministry. He was the one sitting closest to Jesus at the Last Supper (see John 13:23) and the one Jesus asked to watch over his mother, Mary, as he was dying on the cross (see 19:26–27). Most scholars believe this Gospel was written around AD 85–90, which would make it the final biblical account of the life, death, and resurrection of Jesus. This account is filled with passion and Jesus' rich theology. If you want to learn what Jesus said about himself, dig deep into the Gospel of John.

THE BIG PICTURE

Sometimes a movie, story, or book can be confusing. We get to the end and have no idea what the point really was. We scratch our heads and wonder, *What was the message?*

When we read the John's Gospel from beginning to end, the purpose of this Holy Spirit-breathed record of the life of Jesus becomes crystal clear. John, the author of this beautiful account of the Messiah's coming, life, death, and resurrection, sums up his intentions so we can't possibly get the wrong idea. Here is the big picture of John's telling of the Jesus story in his own words:

> *Jesus performed many other signs in the presence of his disciples, which are not recorded in this book. But these are written that you may believe that Jesus is the Messiah, the Son of God, and that by believing you may have life in his name.* (John 20:30–31)

John's Gospel is meant to help people believe that Jesus is exactly who he said he was: the Messiah, the Son of God. John was selective in what accounts he recorded. If he had tried to write down everything that Jesus said and did, his Gospel could have been longer than the Bible itself. Instead, led by the Holy Spirit, John recorded specific signs, teachings, and accounts with the express purpose of helping people truly believe in Jesus.

Then John took things one huge step further. He let the readers of his Gospel (including you and me) know that what we believe about Jesus will transform our lives. When we sincerely believe in the Savior, we have life in his name—not just an ordinary life, but the fullest life possible (see John 10:10).

The purpose of John's Gospel is no mystery. God desires each of us to believe in Jesus and embrace the truth of who he is. Our Creator is delighted when our belief in Jesus transforms our lives. As you begin this forty-day journey through the book of John, pause and pray that your belief will deepen and your life will be transformed by the Word of the living God.

EPIC THEMES

There are many themes in the Gospel of John that are worthy of our focus. Some of these include:

Why Jesus came. Jesus came so that we could believe in him—really believe! Faith in Jesus is the most important thing for any Christian. John could have included many other things about Jesus' life in his Gospel, but he was led by the Spirit to include the things he did so that his readers would believe in Jesus as the Messiah and that by believing would receive the eternal life that God offers to all (see John 20:30–31).

Who Jesus is. If you studied the book of John and highlighted every name for Jesus (that he used of himself, the Father attributed to him, or others used for him), you would get great insight into who our Savior is. In John we find the seven "I am" statements Jesus made of himself. One of the central themes of this Gospel is understanding exactly who Jesus is:

- the Bread of Life (see 6:35, 41, 48, 51)
- the Light of the World (see 8:12)
- the Gate for the sheep (see 10:7–9)
- the Resurrection and the Life (see 11:25)
- the Good Shepherd (see 10:11, 14)

- the Way, the Truth, and the Life (see 14:6)
- the True Vine (see 15:1, 5)
- bonus: the Great I Am (see 8:58 and Exodus 3:14)

What Jesus taught. John recorded a series of extended discourses of Jesus. As the following list shows, some of them are connected to Jesus' teaching about himself while others grew out of the miracles and signs he did:

- new birth (see John 3)
- water of life (see John 4)
- divine Son (see John 5)
- Bread of Life see (see John 6)
- life-giving Spirit (see John 7)
- Light of the World (see John 8)
- Good Shepherd (see John 10)
- Farewell Discourse (see John 14–17)

The miracles Jesus did. The disciple John connected the miracles (or signs) of Jesus to the person of Jesus and often to the teaching of Jesus. Here are some of Jesus' miracles John that records in his Gospel:

- turning water into wine (see 2:1–11)
- healing the official's son (see 4:46–54)
- healing the man at the pool (see 5:1–15)
- feeding the five thousand (see 6:1–13)
- walking on the water (see 6:16–21)
- healing the man born blind (see 9:1–34)
- raising Lazarus from the dead (see 11:38–44)

The sacrifice, death, and resurrection of Jesus. The epic conclusion of John's Gospel is the crucifixion, burial, victorious resurrection, and the post-resurrection appearances of Jesus. This portion of the Gospel reveals that all believers can put their faith in Jesus and that what Jesus promised is absolutely true (see John 19-21).

In a world of doubting and skepticism, Jesus came to help us believe in what matters most—him! When we truly believe in Jesus, he offers us life. In the Savior, we find the meaning of life, abundant life and eternal life. This study of the story of Jesus is meant to do exactly what John said two thousand years ago—help you encounter the Messiah and find life (of every good kind) in his name.

THE WORD BECAME FLESH

JOHN 1

What we believe impacts every aspect of our lives. When God entered human history and the Word became flesh, the power of heaven was unleashed on the earth. God became a man. People could see and believe in him in a whole new way. It is time to ask the question, "What do I really believe about Jesus, and how should this shape my daily life?"

WELCOME

Our lives will be shaped and dramatically impacted by what we believe and where we put our trust. Jesus offers a rock-solid foundation for life. Sadly, many people look to the things of this world and hope they will provide the security and stability their souls long for. Too often the results are tragic.

Countless people have lost their life's savings by getting sucked into an investment scam or Ponzi scheme. They put all the money they have saved into an opportunity that seems too good to be true—because it is! When the truth finally comes out, their retirement savings are gone and there is often nothing they can do to recover their resources.

Many young people have a sense of invincibility. They place their trust in their own strength, abilities, and creativity. Over time the weight of life becomes too much and something has to give. Their blind confidence becomes flooded by uncertainty.

Your soulmate is out there! Just find the right one! So many people spend their lives looking for the perfect person who will "complete them" and make life wonderful. Many never find that elusive prize. Those who do, with time, tend to discover one of two things. That person is not as perfect as they imagined (and sometimes they start looking again). Or the weight and expectations they heap on that one "flawless person" is too much and it crushes them.

If we place our ultimate belief and trust in finances, health, people, or anything else, in time we will end up disappointed, and the sheer weight of life will bring things crumbling down. In the beginning of John's Gospel, we are offered a place to put out trust, belief, hope, and life. Well, it's not really a place; it's a person. He is the Word of God. The Light. The Messiah. Jesus.

SHARE

Tell about a time when you put your hope, trust, or belief in something (or someone), and things did not turn out well.

WATCH

Play the video for session one. (Play the DVD or see the instructions on the inside front cover on how to access the sessions through streaming.) As you watch, use the following outline to record any thoughts, questions, or key points that stand out to you.

The big picture—snapshots of the four Gospels:

- Matthew:
- Mark:
- Luke:
- John:

The focal point of John's Gospel and his big themes:

Jesus the Logos (John 1:1)

- Greek meaning:

- Jewish meaning:

The Word became flesh (John 1:14–18).

What do you really believe?

What do you believe about Jesus?

The number seven in Scripture

The importance of real, growing, and increasing belief in Jesus

Our lives and prayers tell the story of what we believe about everything, including Jesus.

DISCUSS

Take a few minutes to discuss with your group members what you just watched and to explore these concepts in Scripture. Use the following questions to help guide your discussion.

I. What impacted you the most as you watched Kyle's teaching on John 1?

2. **Read John 20:30–31.** Kyle told a story about his son using a walker after an injury. What are some of the "walkers" people use to help them get through life, move forward, and bear the weight that life can heap on them? How has true belief in Jesus helped you (or someone close to you) stand strong and press forward through the hard times of life?

3. **Read John 1:1–5.** This power-packed passage launches us into John's Gospel. Jesus is the "Word." What do we learn about our Savior? how should this impact our belief in him?

4. **Read John 1:14–18.** What do you learn about Jesus (the Word) from this passage? How have you experienced both the grace and truth of Jesus as your belief in him has deepened over time?

5. Our core beliefs shape our attitudes, govern our emotional world, guide our behavior, regulate our relationships, and form our future. Take a moment and write down two or three things that you believe about Jesus at the core of your being. Share one of these beliefs with your group and illustrate how this belief impacts how you walk through life.

6. What are ways we can be sure we are growing to really believe in Jesus and not just gather information about him? How can we help the next generation encounter Jesus so they truly believe in him?

MEMORIZE

In each session, you will be given a key verse (or verses) to memorize from the passage covered in the video teaching. This week your memory verse is John 1:1:

> *In the beginning was the Word, and the Word was with God, and the Word was God.*

Recite this verse out loud. Ask for volunteers who would like to say the verse from memory.

RESPOND

What will you take away from this session? What is one practical next step you can take that will deepen your belief in Jesus and impact your life in a positive way that honors God?

PRAY

Close your group time by praying in any of these directions:

- Lift up prayers of thanks and praise for how Jesus has been the one to strengthen and protect you in the hard times of life.
- Praise God for who Jesus is and for how his presence and power in your life have transformed your past and your present.
- Ask the Holy Spirit to grow your faith in Jesus over the coming forty days, and pray for the members of your group to go deeper in their belief in Jesus.

SESSION ONE

Reflect on the material you have covered in this session by engaging in the following between-session learning resources. Each week you will begin by reviewing the key verse(s) to memorize for the session. During the next six days, you will have an opportunity to read a portion of John's Gospel and reflect on what you learn, respond by taking action, journal some of your insights, and pray about what God has taught you. Finally, on the last day, you will review the key verse(s) and reflect on what you have learned for the week.

DAY 1

Memorize: Begin this week's personal study by reciting the following verse found in John 1:1:

> *In the beginning was the Word, and the Word was with God, and the Word was God.*

Now try to say the verse from memory.

Reflect: The opening chapter of John's Gospel is the Christmas story from very a unique perspective. Matthew records the journey of magi (wise men) coming to Bethlehem with gifts for the newborn King. Luke tells about the encounter the shepherds had with angels in a field at night and their pilgrimage to see Mary, Joseph, and the baby in a manger. But in John's Gospel, we meet the Word of God who "became flesh and made his dwelling among us" (John 1:14). That is his version of the Christmas story. Reflect on the meaning and message that John brings to the incarnation—the coming of God into space and time. Think about John's unique contribution to the story of Jesus entering into our world and lives.

DAY 2

Read: John 1:1–18

Reflect: Grace and truth, that's how Jesus came! As John tells his Christmas story, he is emphatic that Jesus entered our world with overflowing grace and truth (see verse 14). This balance is essential and can be seen in Jesus all through John's Gospel. Grace with no truth can become sentimental pablum with no foundations or boundaries for life. Truth with no grace becomes inflexible dogmatism when doctrine is emphasized but kindness is nowhere to be seen. Grace and truth together can change that world, and that's what Jesus came to do. We should all ask ourselves, *Do I live with a healthy balance of grace and truth?*

Journal:

- What are some of the truths that Jesus spoke and lived that you need to develop more fully in your life?
- Where do you need to develop grace in your heart and extend it to others as you walk through life? How has Jesus been an example to you in these areas?

Pray: Thank Jesus for the grace he has shown to you throughout your life. Pray for a heart that is growing in his grace. Ask for the power of the Holy Spirit to help you show and share grace everywhere you go.

DAY 3

Read: John 1:19–42 and 3:22–36

Reflect: Humility is in short supply in our world. The story of John the Baptist awakens our souls to the beauty and power of a humble heart and life. When the Jewish leaders, a powerful group of influencers, asked John if he was someone of great religious significance (the Messiah, the prophet, or Elijah), he gave an honest and simple no. He then went on to explain that his role was to point to the Messiah, lift him up, and help people see him. This was not a case of self-hatred or poor self-esteem; it was the pure truth. John came as a messenger. He was a signpost firmly placed in the dirt of this world, pointing "This way to Jesus!" This was enough for John. He delighted in the privilege. How is humility growing in your life today?

Journal:
- What are signs and indicators that you are increasing in pride and becoming absorbed in your glory instead of focusing on Jesus?
- What are specific steps you can take to become humbler in heart and actions?

Pray: Ask the Spirit of God to open your eyes to ways that pride might be growing in your heart and life. Confess these to God and ask for power to repent and turn from pride. Ask for Jesus to help you walk in humility as you do all you can to put him first and point others to the Savior and not yourself.

DAY 4

Read: John 1:43–51

Reflect: Jesus saw you long before you recognized and followed him. In Nathanael's story, we meet a man who was amazed that Jesus saw him and knew him even before they met. The closer we follow the Savior and the more we learn about the God who made us, the less surprised we will be at his sovereign work in our lives. God knows everything about us yet still loves us. In the depths of our sin and rebellion, Jesus knew us and was willing to die in our place for our sins. We should never be shocked at how much God knows about us, for he is omniscient (he knows all things) and nothing escapes his view. What should amaze us is that God loves us and lavishes us with his grace even when he knows our whole stories! Do you know that you have absolutely no secrets from God?

Journal:
- God knows *everything* about you. What are some of the implications when we realize we have no secrets from God?
- How does God's omniscience (ability to know all things) deepen your faith and shape what you believe about Jesus?

Pray: Praise God for his sovereign power and omniscient glory. Thank him for knowing everything about you yet still loving you and offering you cleansing through Jesus. Pray for a daily awareness that God's loving eyes never wander from you and his presence never leaves you.

DAY 5

Read: John 2:1–12

Reflect: Jesus' turning water into wine was the first of his seven signs (recorded in John's Gospel) that revealed who he was and helped people believe in him. You might wonder, *How in the world does making wine—really good wine—help people believe in Jesus?* The point is not found in the wine but in the meaning behind this miracle. Of course it is impressive and a disruption of the normal biological process for someone to change water into wine, but more is happening. When the master of the banquet said, "But you have saved the best till now" (verse 10), he was getting to the heart of the miracle. Jesus was the fulfillment of all the Old Testament messianic prophecies. He was the better and perfected version of all that had come before (in the book of Hebrews this comes up over and over). He would be the final sacrifice as well as the perfect High Priest, and he would do what no one or nothing before him could. When you see Jesus and believe in him, you learn that the best was saved for last!

Journal:
- How has Jesus satisfied you and filled you with what your heart and life longed for?
- What are some of the possible consequences and dangers of looking to other things or people to give you meaning and satisfaction in life?

Pray: Thank your heavenly Father for sending Jesus, his beloved Son, as the final sacrifice and full payment for all of your sins. Give praise to Jesus for his miracle-working power in ancient times and in your life today. Ask the Holy Spirit to help you notice all the ways Jesus is still the best of all you need in this world and for eternity.

DAY 6

Read: John 3:1–21

Reflect: We all have our own unique and Spirit-led journey to Jesus. For Nicodemus, one of the most powerful and influential religious leaders in his community, his search for Jesus began in the dark. He was spiritually blind, which is an odd thing to say about a religious elite. He also came to Jesus under the cloak of darkness. He came at night because he did not want others in his community to recognize that he was seeking to learn from Jesus. But as Nicodemus talked with Jesus, listened, and entered into some rabbinical argumentation, the light of Jesus began to break through. With time, Nicodemus placed his belief in Jesus and was transformed. What was your journey to Jesus? How did he meet you where you were and lead you to faith in his name?

Journal:
- What have you learned about Jesus in his interaction with Nicodemus, and how does this connect with your journey to the Savior?

- How was Nicodemus's path to faith unique, and what are some of the distinctive aspects of your own faith journey?

Pray: Thank God for the unique ways he has drawn your heart to the Lord. Pray for people you love who are not yet Jesus followers, asking God to meet them where they are and draw them to himself. Praise God that he is willing to meet us in the day or the night, in times of joy or sorrow.

DAY 7

Memorize: Conclude this week's personal study by again reciting John 1:1:

> *In the beginning was the Word, and the Word was with God, and the Word was God.*

Now try to say the verse from memory.

Reflect: Jesus was divine! He was not just a great teacher. He was more than a gifted and popular rabbi. He was a miracle worker, but this was not the whole story. Jesus was infinity wrapped in human flesh. Divinity in diapers. God with us. Why must the tenet that Jesus was fully divine be central to our belief? Take time to reflect on Jesus' divine attributes and thank him for accomplishing for us what we could never do on our own.

GRACE FOR THE OUTCAST

JOHN 4

We naturally want to run and hide when our sins come into the light where everyone can see them, causing us to feel embarrassed and ashamed. Children, seniors, and others in between have the same response. In these moments when we feel outcast and unworthy, God comes looking for us. When our false assumptions push us away from God, our Savior brings the truth and speaks it with grace. If we are ready to hear, he is always ready to speak.

WELCOME

It's a simple and common childhood rite of passage. It begins when someone explains the game. The rules are simple. First, I cover my eyes and count to a number (providing just enough time for you to quickly scurry to find a good hiding place). Second, you run and hide. Third, I try my best to find you.

That's about it.

Coming up with a name for this game did not demand a marketing team or great innovation process. It's called hide-and-seek. Most kids can learn the game in about three minutes.

The sad reality is that we can end up playing this game long past childhood. It takes on many forms, but if we are not careful, we can spend a lifetime hiding from friends, family, strangers, our boss, and even God.

An employee begins to cut corners at work, and he does not really give his best effort or work all of his assigned hours. Then he discovers he can take small items from the workplace without anyone noticing. He assures himself, *No one will really care or find out.* With time he ends up embezzling and living with the constant anxiety and fear of getting caught. Over months and years, he hides, covers up, and does all he can to be sure his tracks are never seen. While he hides, God is still seeking.

A wife enters into a flirtatious relationship with a neighbor. *It means nothing*, she tells herself. But with time, flirting becomes long and intimate conversations when no one else is around. Without thinking about the consequences, she allows a late-night liaison to evolve into inappropriate intimacy and begins concealing the evidence, covering her tracks, and hiding her heart from the man she married more than a decade ago. While she hides, God sees and seeks her out.

A student begins cheating now and then and becomes reliant on other people's schoolwork to keep his grades up. He knows it's wrong, but what can he do now? It seems too late to trust in his own mind and work—it's easier to cheat. His life becomes a game of hiding from teachers, parents, and anyone who might catch on. While he hides, the God who loves him seeks out this young man, wanting him to make things right.

Hiding is a natural response when we recognize our own shortcomings and sins. But this is no game. The God of heaven has done all that needs to be done to make us whole and bring us into his light. When we feel outcast and far from God, his grace comes knocking on our door.

SHARE

Tell about a time in your childhood or teenage years when you found yourself hiding something from others—even God. What did this process of hiding feel like?

WATCH

Play the video for session two. As you watch, use the following outline to record any thoughts, questions, or key points that stand out to you.

A modern-day story of stains and hiding:

A biblical account of stains and hiding:

○ Jesus had to go through Samaria (John 4:4–6).

- ○ Jesus and the woman have a conversation about water (John 4:7–15).

- ○ A deeper story begins to surface (John 4:16–18).

- ○ The woman tries to redirect the conversation—she tries to hide from Jesus (John 4:19–26).

Three false assumptions about Jesus:

I. Jesus wants nothing to do with me.

2. Jesus is more interested in religion than in me.

3. Jesus makes an offer that is simply too good to be true.

Jesus tells the woman who he is (the Messiah), and she believes.

We can tell others our story of encountering Jesus and his forgiveness and grace.

DISCUSS

Take a few minutes to discuss with your group members what you just watched and to explore these concepts in Scripture. Use the following questions to help guide your discussion.

1. What impacted you the most as you watched Kyle's teaching on John 4?

2. **Read John 4:4–15.** What was this woman thinking when Jesus talked about "living water," and what was Jesus trying to get her to understand about himself (the true Living Water)? Why do you think there was so much underlying tension and confusion in this conversation?

3. **Read John 4:16–18.** What are some of the reasons this woman might have thought Jesus had no interest in her? What are some lies Satan tells us, or that we might tell

ourselves, that cause us to hide from God and feel like he doesn't care about us?

4. **Read John 4:19–24.** How did the woman try to spin the conversation away from herself and toward theology and religion? What are ways we can get caught up in religious talk or activity in an effort to avoid facing the deep soul issues that Jesus says matter the most?

5. What are some reasons this woman might have been cynical and cautious about the gift Jesus was offering? What are some lies we tell ourselves (or others tell us) that can make us feel that what Jesus offers is simply too good to be true?

6. **Read John 4:28–30.** Kyle's daughter was amazed by grace when the forgiveness of her stain became a symbol of love. When this happened, she just had to tell others about it! How has Jesus cleansed your stains, loved you radically, and given you a fresh start in life? Who is one person you want to share the story of your journey from guilt to grace with, and how can your group members pray as you seek to do this?

MEMORIZE

Your memory verse this week is from John 4:14:

> *"Whoever drinks the water I give them will never thirst.*
> *Indeed, the water I give them will become in them a spring*
> *of water welling up to eternal life."*

Recite this verse out loud. Ask for volunteers who would like to say the verse from memory.

RESPOND

What will you take away from this session? What is one practical next step you can take to share the hope, love, truth, and grace of Jesus with someone who is still far from the Savior?

PRAY

Close your group time by praying in any of these directions:

- Thank Jesus for how he calls out to the outcasts in this world (including each of us) and draws them to himself.
- Pray that you and your group members will identify any lies about Jesus that might be lingering in your hearts or in your lives.
- Ask the Holy Spirit to give you boldness to tell others how Jesus has removed your shame and guilt and replaced it with love and confidence in him.

SESSION TWO

Reflect on the material you have covered in this session by engaging in the following between-session learning resources. Each week you will begin by reviewing the key verse(s) to memorize for the session. During the next six days, you will have an opportunity to read a portion of John's Gospel and reflect on what you learn, respond by taking action, journal some of your insights, and pray about what God has taught you. Finally, on the last day, you will review the key verse(s) and reflect on what you have learned for the week.

DAY 8

Memorize: Begin this week's personal study by reciting the following verse found in John 4:14:

> *"Whoever drinks the water I give them will never thirst. Indeed, the water I give them will become in them a spring of water welling up to eternal life."*

Now try to say the verse from memory.

Reflect: Remember where Jesus was having this conversation with the Samaritan woman. They were in a desert, sitting by a well. In that part of the world water was life, and a lack of water could mean death. Jesus was promising a never-ending, thirst-quenching source of water. The problem was that the woman was thinking only about *physical* water. Jesus wanted her to recognize that her thirst for *spiritual* water was actually greater than her need for physical water. This is also true for us. Think about how your relationship with Jesus helped to quench the deep longings of your soul. Thank him for being the Living Water who satisfies your greatest needs.

DAY 9

Read: John 2:13–23

Reflect: Jesus always invites outsiders in. When Jesus walked the earth, the temple in Jerusalem was the primary gathering place for people to come and meet with God. Because the temple was the hub of Jewish worship, there was one special place where non-Jewish worshipers could come and join in— the Court of the Gentiles. Take a wild guess at what part of the temple had become a market for selling animals and exchanging foreign currency so people could give offerings. You got it: the courtyard of the Gentiles. It was so crowded, loud, and filled with commerce that the non-Jewish people who came from all around the world had no place to actually worship

God. Jesus would have none of this. He loves to make space for outsiders to come and feel welcome. So he cleaned house!

Journal:
- What do you learn about the heart of Jesus and his passion for people from every nation to draw near God as you read this passage?
- What are some of the practices, systems, and forms of church life that get in the way of "outsiders" feeling welcome in our churches? What can we do to overturn and drive these out?

Pray: Thank Jesus for his deep love and passion for the outcast and forgotten in this world. Pray for your church to remove unnecessary things that get in the way of guests experiencing the presence, truth, and grace of God.

DAY 10

Read: John 4:1–42

Reflect: Jesus meets us where we are. This is true both physically and spiritually. Think about it: The Samaritan woman was hiding in the heat of the day. She avoided the cool of the morning when everyone else came to draw water. But Jesus was on a mission. He came and found her right where she was, at just the right time. Even more powerful was how Jesus met her spiritual needs and spoke in ways that connected for her. As you pray for lost people and seek to shine the light of Jesus, are you ready to meet them right where they are?

Journal:
- Write down the names of a few people you care about who are not yet followers of Jesus. Where do they hang out? If you are going to connect with them on their own turf, where will that be?
- Now go a bit deeper. What are their spiritual questions? What lies do they believe that keep them from Jesus? How can you meet them where they are on their spiritual journey and help them take steps closer to Jesus?

Pray: Thank God that he met you right where you were and drew you to the heart of Jesus. Invite the Holy Spirit to give you courage and wisdom to meet lost and wandering people where they are and help them move closer to Jesus, the Savior.

DAY II

Read: John 4:43–54

Reflect: We can and should take God at his word. In this account, a father came to Jesus with an appeal to heal his sick son. His boy was knocking on death's door, and this royal official had confidence that if Jesus would come and minister to him, there was hope for healing. Jesus did not agree to travel to this man's home; he simply said, "Your son will live." What happened next was beautiful! The official "took Jesus at his word and departed." He just believed. He was confident in what Jesus said. And on his way home, he got word that his son was healed at the very moment Jesus declared it would be so. We should live with bold confidence in the words of Jesus—do you?

Journal:
- What are some of the truths and promises that Jesus spoke in the Scriptures? Make a list. (Note: Be sure your list items are actually promises made in Scripture and not your own desires or ideas you want to impose on Jesus.)
- What are steps you can take to live in ways that reflect your confidence in these promises of Jesus?

Pray: Thank Jesus that his words are always true. Give him praise for promises he has kept throughout your life. Ask for fresh boldness to read, know, believe, and live confidently in the promises he has given.

DAY 12

Read: John 6:1–15

Reflect: When Jesus touches and blesses anything, it can multiply. Andrew asked a powerful question in the middle of this biblical narrative. The disciples had figured out the basic math and the sheer impossibility of feeding all of the people who had gathered to listen to Jesus preach. If they had cash that was equal to half a year's wages (and it looked like they did not), then they could go shopping for food, bring back carts and carts of fresh bread, cut it up, and then almost everyone could have one bite. Get the picture? On the heels of this realization, Andrew brought forth a boy's lunch of five small barley loaves and two small fish but asked, "But how far will they go among so many?" We know the answer. When something is placed in the hands of Jesus, lifted up, and blessed, it will go as far as is needed. Do you live with a bold confidence that Jesus has the ability to bless and multiply the things you give over to him?

Journal:
- What are ways that you have surrendered things to Jesus in the past, and how has he shown up, provided things, multiplied things, and amazed you?

• What is something you are holding on to but need to release to Jesus so that he can do what only he can?

Pray: Thank God for all he has blessed you with. Ask the Holy Spirit to show you things you are clinging to that you need to place in Jesus' hands. Pray for God's multiplying power to be unleashed in your life.

DAY 13

Read: John 6:25–71

Reflect: There is bread and there is Bread. After multiplying bread for the masses and taking a walk on the water, Jesus went deeper into the topic of bread. He taught about the desert wandering of the people of Israel and reminded his hearers that God provided bread from heaven (manna) in one of their greatest times of need. Many who were listening to Jesus were present when he had taken a handful of dinner rolls and fed thousands of people—and they'd even seen the leftovers! So now they wanted more bread. They wanted Jesus to set up shop and get baking. Make bread for the masses, and they will love you. Jesus' message was simple but life-changing: there is bread and there is Bread. There is physical bread you eat and digest, and then you will be hungry again. There is also spiritual Bread (Jesus the Bread of Life). When you partake of him, you will never hunger again. What are most people interested in, bread or Bread?

Journal:
- What are ways that your belief in Jesus and relationship with him satisfy your greatest hunger and quench your deepest spiritual thirst?
- How can you feast more on your relationship with Jesus and find satisfaction in what he offers you every day?

Pray: Thank Jesus for the daily physical bread (and other material blessings) that he provides for you. Pray for a heart and life that longs more and more for the spiritual blessings Jesus offers and less and less for the physical and transitory things our world promises.

DAY 14

Memorize: Conclude this week's personal study by again reciting John 4:14:

> *"Whoever drinks the water I give them will never thirst. Indeed, the water I give them will become in them a spring of water welling up to eternal life."*

Reflect: When we are filled with the living water of Jesus, we actually overflow. Because Jesus fills us and fills us and fills us, his presence, grace, love, and truth well up inside of us and we can't hold it back. Think about some of the people in your life who are still living in a spiritual desert. How can you sprinkle or pour out the life-saving water you have received from the Savior? Take time to pray for courage and wisdom as you tell people you love about the life-giving water you have received from Jesus.

GRACE FOR THE BROKEN

JOHN 5

Jesus encountered all sorts of broken people when he walked on this earth. He loved to stop, talk, listen, and extend grace in many shapes and forms. When people believed in him, the windows of heaven opened up and God's blessings poured out. Broken people still find healing, hope, and a future when faith takes hold and they learn to walk in the ways of the Savior.

WELCOME

Are you hopeful or hopeless? The answer to this question will impact every part of your life. When a person has belief and expectation that God is near, that he cares, and that he is ready to help, a light shines in their life and in their eyes. When the same person feels hopeless because they believe God is uncaring or unable to help, life becomes dark.

Imagine a married couple who is celebrating their twenty-fifth anniversary. They have had a quarter century filled with both great memories and deeply painful moments. They have raised and launched a son and daughter who are doing quite well. Their daughter is expecting twins, and they are excited about meeting their first grandchildren. They also carry the pain of losing their firstborn son in a tragic accident when he was only fourteen years old. They get along most of the time but also lock horns on some of the same issues that have caused marital tension for two and a half decades. They are much like most couples with a mixed bag of joys and sorrow as they walk through life together.

What could their future look like if they believed God had plans for them that are good and meaningful? What power might they draw from the throne of heaven if they lived with daily hope that God loved to be near them and to guide their steps, even on the rough terrain of this world? How might their marriage, family, and all of their life together be infused with hope and joy if they walked each step profoundly confident that God is on the throne and ready to move powerfully in their lives? What good things could happen if they partnered with their heavenly Father and did all they could, in the power of the Holy Spirit, to follow and serve Jesus?

Now imagine the same couple in the same landmark season of life. What would happen if they both focused all their attention on the pain of the past and the losses they had faced? What would their future look like if each of them (secretly in their heart) began giving up on each other and their life together? What if they believed that God was not near, did not care, or lacked the power to help them even if he wanted to? What might their marriage and lives look like in a year or five years from now?

Our beliefs impact our today and our tomorrow. When we believe in Jesus, really believe, our faith permeates all of life. When our beliefs move us to action, the power of heaven is unleashed and hope becomes reality.

SHARE

Tell about a time when you were feeling discouraged or hopeless or had a crisis of faith. Describe how Jesus showed up and grew your faith and belief in him.

WATCH

Play the video for session three. As you watch, use the following outline to record any thoughts, questions, or key points that stand out to you.

Why John wrote his Gospel and two questions (John 20:30–31)

Some people don't believe.

   ○ Some prefer darkness to light (John 3:19).

- o Some are afraid of what others will think of them
  (John 7:12–13).

An example of belief that captures the heart, mind, and all of life

An overview of the seven signs (miracles) in John's Gospel

1.

2.

3.

4.

5.

6.

7.

Thirty-eight years of waiting and a new beginning started with belief (John 5:1–15).

- o Background on the location (the pool of Bethesda)

- o Sometimes discouragement sets in and hope moves out.

- o Do you want to be healed?

Three honest questions:

- o Do you believe things in your life can change?

- o Do you believe Jesus wants to help you?

- o What keeps you from believing?

DISCUSS

Take a few minutes to discuss with your group members what
you just watched and to explore these concepts in Scripture.
Use the following questions to help guide your discussion.

1. What impacted you the most as you watched Kyle's teaching
   on John 5?

2. **Read John 3:19–20.** Why do many people run to the
   darkness of this world rather than toward the light of Jesus?
   What are some of the dark places people are enticed to run
   toward in our world today?

3. **Read John 7:12–13.** The Gospels recite numerous examples of
   people who moved away from Jesus because they feared what
   other people might think. How does our present culture lend
   itself to erosion of belief in Jesus and decreasing commitment
   to God's Word and truth? How can we stand strong in our
   beliefs even when doing so is costly and unpopular?

4. **Read** John 5:1–8. After thirty-eight years of continued sick-
   ness, how might the man at the pool have been feeling? Why
   do you think Jesus asked him, "Do you want to get well?"
   Why is the answer to this question so important?

5. What causes some people (both followers of Jesus and nonbelievers) to question if things in their lives can actually change for the better? What would Jesus say to someone who was living in the lie that things can never get better?

6. Some people, both Christians and non-Christians, have a hard time realizing that God loves them so much that he wants to draw near and strengthen them. They don't believe they are worthy of the love and help of Jesus. With what you know of the heart of the Savior and the teaching of the Scriptures, what would you say to someone who believes the lie that Jesus does not want to help them? Pray for open doors to share this good news with someone in the coming days.

MEMORIZE

Your memory verse this week is from John 5:6:

When Jesus saw him lying there and learned that he had been in this condition for a long time, he asked him, "Do you want to get well?"

Recite this verse out loud. Ask for volunteers who would like to say the verse from memory.

RESPOND

What will you take away from this session? What is one practical step you can take to increase your faith in the middle of hard times, seasons of waiting, and moments of discouragement?

PRAY

Close your group time by praying in any of these directions:

- Pray for people in your life whom you care about and who resist belief in Jesus because they love darkness or are afraid to count the cost of following Jesus.
- Thank Jesus for the miracles and signs he did when he walked on this earth, and thank him also for the ways he is still working in power today.
- Ask God to grow the faith of your group members so that you all live with hope and are always ready to partner with God as your beliefs move you to action.

SESSION THREE

Reflect on the material you have covered in this session by engaging in the following between-session learning resources. Each week you will begin by reviewing the key verse(s) to memorize for the session. During the next six days, you will have an opportunity to read a portion of John's Gospel and reflect on what you learn, respond by taking action, journal some of your insights, and pray about what God has taught you. Finally, on the last day, you will review the key verse(s) and reflect on what you have learned for the week.

DAY 15

Memorize: Begin this week's personal study by reciting the following verse found in John 5.6.

> When Jesus saw him lying there and learned that he had been in this condition for a long time, he asked him, "Do you want to get well?"

Now try to say the verse from memory.

Reflect: This man was flat out of gas! For almost four decades he had been in the same spot, waiting for the water to stir, bubble, or do anything that would indicate it was time to jump in. By this point, you can only imagine his discouragement. Not once had he entered the water and experienced any kind of change in his physical condition. It was at this moment that Jesus showed up. Think about any situation you have in your life that is causing you to feel stuck, discouraged, or helpless. Look up. Look around. Jesus is near.

DAY 16

Read: John 5:1–15

Reflect: Jesus needed no spells, incantations, performance art, or hoopla. The man by the pool clung to superstition for thirty-eight years. A variety of ideas have been set forth concerning this particular pool, but the general consensus is that when the water stirred (maybe moved by a passing angel or some unknown power), the first one in the water got healing. You would think that close to four decades of trying would have gotten the job done, but when Jesus showed up, he did not help roll the guy into the pool at just the right moment. Instead, Jesus simply said, "Get up! Pick up your mat and walk." No smoke bombs, no lengthy speeches, no flash or flare. Jesus did not need to put on a show—he was God. His word had created the heavens and the earth. When you look to Jesus and cry out for his help, don't look for a show—look to Jesus the Savior.

Journal:
- Make a list of a few times you have experienced Jesus' presence, provision, comfort, touch, or healing. How did he move and work in your life?
- What are some places you (or someone you care about) need the touch of Jesus and his power unleashed in your life? Make a list and lift each of these before the Savior, who has all power in the universe.

Pray: Spend time praying for yourself and your small group members. Ask for Jesus, the one who only needs to say the word and heavenly power is unleashed, and trust him to move according to his will and wisdom.

DAY 17

Read: John 5:16–30

Reflect: Jesus was not looking to pick a fight. He was just being clear about who he was. The Jewish leaders got the message. This traveling rabbi (whom they saw as a troublemaker) was calling himself God. He was claiming to be equal with Yahweh. There were really only two logical responses to the claims of Jesus: (1) declare that he was a heretic and get rid of him, or (2) fall down and worship him. Two thousand years late, we still have only these two options.

Journal:
- What did Jesus say in this passage that clarified who he was?
- How did the Jewish leaders miss the point and in the process miss the Messiah they claimed to be waiting to meet?

Pray: Lift up prayers of worship, and praise Jesus as the Divine One, God with us, the Savior of the world.

DAY 18

Read: John 5:31–47

Reflect: Reading the Bible does not guarantee authentic belief in Jesus. The religious leaders knew the Word of God (the Old Testament Scriptures), but they did not recognize the *Word* of God (Jesus) standing right in front of them. What irony! Jesus explained that even though they were scholars of the book, they had missed the point. One of the central reasons God had breathed his Holy Word was so people would recognize the Messiah when he arrived. They had looked to the Scriptures as the source of eternal life but did not embrace the Savior who brought the life they longed for. As you open the Scriptures day by day, learn from God and always look for Jesus, the source of your life.

Journal:

- Look back over the past couple of weeks to see how much time you spent reading the Scriptures. When do you read the Bible (or listen to it)? What do you read? Be honest and get a sense of your devotion to growing in your knowledge and obedience to God's Word.

- How do you encounter Jesus when you are reading the Bible? Are you simply checking something off your to-do list when you are in the Word, or are you encountering your Savior? How can you go deeper in the Scriptures and make sure you are encountering your living Savior as you do?

Pray: Thank God for inspiring his Holy Word, and pray for growing discipline to read, study, love, and follow the teachings of the Bible.

DAY 19

Read: John 7

Reflect: Don't look for conflict, but don't avoid it either. That seems to have been Jesus' approach to dealing with the religious leaders, political leaders, and even the crowds when they were fired up. Jesus was always ready to respond with clarity and wisdom when things started heating up. Scholars who study the life of Christ refer to a number of accounts in the Gospels as "conflict narratives." These were times when a question about Sabbath observance or some other religious topic would be debated with great zeal by the religious establishment and Jesus. In this chapter, we see this kind of conflict in full force. As always, Jesus kept teaching the truth, speaking with wisdom, and moving forward the kingdom of God.

Journal:
- What are some of the conflicts you might face as you follow Jesus in our increasingly polarized and antagonistic world?
- How can you follow the example of Jesus and not pick fights but be ready to answer people with gracious and bold clarity?

Pray: Pray for a gentle spirit and tongue when you face battles about faith. And ask God to help you be prepared for these tough but needed conversations.

DAY 20

Read: John 8

Reflect: After John 7, we might expect the conflict narratives to be over, but they keep on coming. Jesus declared that he was the "light of the world" (verse 12), and the Pharisees did not like that at all. Jesus said he was "going away" (verse 21), and the religious leaders wondered if he was going to commit suicide. Jesus spoke of knowing the truth and declared that "the truth will set you free" (verse 32), and this led to a discussion about the devil, God, and who was the true father of the religious leaders. By the end of the chapter, we find the religious leaders picking up stones and getting ready to execute Jesus (verse 59). But through all of the conflict, Jesus, the Light of the World, just kept on shining. We need to learn to be more like Jesus when we are misrepresented.

Journal:
- How have you seen Jesus shine his light and bring his presence into your life during dark and hard times?
- What can you learn from Jesus' example in the way you respond when others against you, twist your words, or misrepresent what you have said

Pray: Thank Jesus for being the Light of the World and the one who illuminates your life.

DAY 21

Memorize: Conclude this week's personal study by again reciting John 5:6:

When Jesus saw him lying there and learned that he had been in this condition for a long time, he asked him, "Do you want to get well?"

Reflect: Jesus' question seems almost unkind at first glance. Of course the man wanted to get well; he had been there for just shy of four decades. Certainly he wanted healing—he was close to the pool where this sort of thing was supposed to happen. Undoubtedly he wanted to get better. Why else would he still be there? Yet Jesus, the wisest man who ever lived, asked the question anyway: "Do you want to get well?" Maybe there was more happening than meets the eye. Maybe a declaration of belief and personal engagement were parts of God's plan for true life transformation. When we are stuck, we might do well to ask the same question of ourselves and then answer Jesus with total honesty.

TRUTH FOR THE CLUELESS

JOHN 13

Jesus knows us, loves us, and came to this world to lead us in his ways. When we are wandering and unaware of what it really means to live for God's glory, Jesus not only teaches us but shows us. When we are clueless, our Savior brings the truth in a way that we can see, understand, and live out—for his glory.

WELCOME

Imagine a toddler reaching for a scorching cup of coffee. She is unaware of the pain that awaits her if she plunges her hand into the dark, steaming cup of liquid that looks so inviting. As Dad sees her reach, he moves into action. He removes the coffee and tries to explain. "Hot!" "Ouch!" He even mimes touching the shining liquid and makes a face filled with pain. What is Dad doing? He is trying to bring truth to the clueless.

A military commander holds a weapon in his hands during basic training. Many of the recruits have little to no experience with this particular firearm. Some have no knowledge of how to safely handle any gun. The commander walks through the basics. He is clear, precise, and remedial. His goal is not to insult with simplicity but to save them from the serious consequences of mishandling this weapon. What is he doing? Bringing truth to the clueless.

A surgeon walks the hospital hallways, doing her daily rounds with a small group of doctors in training. She talks about bedside manner, leads them through case studies, and asks question after question. She is making sure they can recognize symptoms, identify hidden causes, make a correct diagnosis, and take the appropriate action. She is relentless and precise. Why is she leaning so hard on these future doctors? They will be making life-and-death decisions, and she wants them to be ready for anything that comes their way. She is bringing truth to the clueless.

The father, military commander, and surgeon all have the best intentions in mind. To the casual observer, they might look tough or harsh. The reality is, each one knows that truth must be imparted and learned. In the same way, the God who made us and loves us seeks to teach his truth so we can follow his ways. This is why it is no surprise that Jesus was often teaching his followers truths they needed to know. Often Jesus' followers were clueless about their need until Jesus showed them.

SHARE

Tell about a time when you learned a biblical truth that was simple and life changing. How did God impart this truth into your heart and life?

WATCH

Play the video for session four. As you watch, use the following outline to record any thoughts, questions, or key points that stand out to you.

King of the Hill—a game and a way of life

The disciples played "King of the Hill," and all of us are tempted to join in (Luke 22:24–28).

A living sermon—washing the disciples' feet (John 13:1–17)

○ Jesus knew who he was (John 13.1–3).

○ Jesus served those who would hurt and abandon him (John 13:4–5).

- Jesus served even in a hard time (John 13:21).

- Jesus served those who were "socially below him."

- Jesus called us to serve like he did (John 13:14–16).

- Jesus gave a "new" command (John 13:34).

- Jesus was clear that serving sends a clear message to the world (John 13:35).

We can misunderstand what will really be a witness to the world.

John, the Gospel writer, experienced radical transformation, and so can we.

DISCUSS

Take a few minutes to discuss with your group members what you just watched and to explore these concepts in Scripture. Use the following questions to help guide your discussion.

1. What impacted you the most as you watched Kyle's teaching on John 13?

2. **Read John 13:1–5.** What did Jesus understand about himself, and how was this directly connected to his willingness to wash the disciples' feet? How should your view of who you are in Christ move you deeper and deeper into a life of humble service?

3. What are some of the ways we are tempted to play "King of the Hill," and why is this in direct opposition to the teaching and example of Jesus?

4. **Read John 13:12–17.** After living out the message, Jesus called his followers to action. If we declare that Jesus is our Teacher and Lord, what should our lives look like

(specifically) as we seek to serve others the way Jesus taught us to serve? Share one way you need to take a step forward in your efforts to serve others in the name of Jesus, and explain how your group members can pray for you and keep you accountable to do it.

5. **Read John 13:34–35.** How can our love for others become a witness to the world that we are really and truly the followers of Jesus? Give an example of how Christians who refuse to love others can become a roadblock to nonbelievers opening their hearts to follow Jesus.

6. In the teaching for today's session, Kyle painted a picture of how John (who was once nicknamed "Son of Thunder") was the one whom Jesus (while dying on the cross) asked to watch over his mother after Jesus was gone. What a beautiful transformation! Share one way God has changed, or is changing, you to be more like his Son as you love, serve, and care for others in the Savior's name.

MEMORIZE

Your memory verses this week are from John 13:14–15:

> *"Now that I, your Lord and Teacher, have washed your feet, you also should wash one another's feet. I have set you an example that you should do as I have done for you."*

Recite these verses out loud. Ask for volunteers who would like to say the verses from memory.

RESPOND

What will you take away from this session? What is one practical step you can take to serve others as Jesus has served you?

PRAY

Close your group time by praying in any of these directions:

- Thank God for coming among us, washing feet, and dying on the cross. Pray that his example of humble service captures your heart and life.
- Pray for each of your group members (by name) to live with a great engagement in serving others with the heart and spirit of Jesus.
- Confess where you have fallen into the pattern of expecting others to serve you, and ask the Spirit of God to show you where you need to repent and change your attitude and actions.

SESSION FOUR

R eflect on the material you have covered in this session by engaging in the following between-session learning resources. Each week you will begin by reviewing the key verse(s) to memorize for the session. During the next six days, you will have an opportunity to read a portion of John's Gospel and reflect on what you learn, respond by taking action, journal some of your insights, and pray about what God has taught you. Finally, on the last day, you will review the key verse(s) and reflect on what you have learned for the week.

DAY 22

Memorize: Begin this week's personal study by reciting the following verses found in John 13:14–15.

> *"Now that I, your Lord and Teacher, have washed your feet, you also should wash one another's feet. I have set you an example that you should do as I have done for you."*

Now try to say the verses from memory.

Reflect: Jesus brings out the big guns in this teaching. He reminds his disciples that he is both their Rabbi and the Lord of their lives. That is what they call him. That is who he is. Jesus did not often use titles (though he had many). But in this setting, he was making a point. He is the Ruler, the Master, the Lord of all—and he washed feet. Think about what you can do to remind yourself regularly that the maker of heaven and earth served you with his own life—and how that reality should shape the way you see your call to serve others.

DAY 23

Read: John 9

Reflect: One of the things we see in this remarkable passage is an example of missing the point. Jesus healed a man born blind. What could be more amazing and exciting? Everyone who heard the story should have been in awe and filled with joy. But the religious leaders of the day used the occasion to attack Jesus on a religious technicality: Jesus had healed the man on the Sabbath. The rabbinical tradition had defined making bricks—out of mud—on the Sabbath as work, so therefore it was a sin. When Jesus healed the man, he "made some mud" and put it on the man's eyes (verse 11). Did you catch that? Jesus made mud. Sounds a lot like work, right? The religious leaders missed a glorious miracle of God because they were consumed with rule keeping. And by the way, it was not an actual Old Testament law, but one of the rules added to help people never even come close to breaking one of God's commandments. Are there ways we still can get caught up in man-made rule following to such an extent that we miss the presence, work, and miracles of God?

Journal:
- What are some of the man-made rules church people can get caught up in that become legalism?
- How can we hold to God's Word but not add our own extra legalism to what the Scriptures teach?

Pray: Thank God for giving us his Word to lead us and set us free. Pray that you will be free from legalism but deeply devoted to following the teachings of Scripture.

DAY 24

Read: John 10

Reflect: Throughout the book of John, we find things in groups of seven. One of these is Jesus' series of seven "I am" declarations. In John 1,0 Jesus makes this bold statement: "I am the good shepherd" (verses 10, 14). He goes on to describe his intimate knowledge of us, his sheep. He is clear that the Shepherd lays his life down for those under his charge. It is staggering and humbling to realize that the Good Shepherd each of us needs is Jesus, God with us, the Messiah. We should live each day aware and amazed that we are the sheep of his pasture.

Journal:
- What are some of the things a good shepherd does for the members of his flock, and what does that mean for you as Jesus' sheep?
- How should your awareness that you are a sheep under the watchful care of Jesus impact the way you walk through each day on this planet?

Pray: Take time to read and pray through Psalm 23.

DAY 25

Read: John 11

Reflect: Jesus is the resurrection and the life. In John 11 we find another of Jesus' seven "I am" sayings (see verse 25). The Savior was talking with Martha, a dear friend, who was mourning the recent death of her brother, Lazarus. He had been in the tomb for three days, and Martha boldly declared that she was confident her brother would be raised at the last day. Jesus gave a whole new perspective. He told her that the power of resurrection was standing right in front of her. He was and is the resurrection. What happened next was glorious! Jesus spoke the word, and Lazarus came back to life. Martha had good theology, but Jesus reminded her that he was the source of life.

Journal:

- In Jesus' raising Lazarus to life, we get a foretaste of his resurrection power. When Jesus rose again and walked out of the tomb, breaking the power of sin, death, Satan, and hell, he gave us a whole new perspective on his authority over the grave. What does the resurrecting power of Jesus mean for us who follow him as our Savior and the Leader of our lives?
- How have you experienced the resurrection power of Jesus in your life?

Pray: Lift up praise to Jesus for his victory over sin and death. Ask for a renewed awareness that you can walk in the power of Jesus' resurrection every day of your life.

DAY 26

Read: John 12

Reflect: In John 12, a series of events point to the sober reality that Jesus was nearing the end of his life on earth. Mary anointed Jesus, and he was clear that this stunning act of generosity was part of preparing him for burial (see verses 1–11). Jesus entered Jerusalem to cries of "Hosanna!" and the waving of palm branches (see verses 12–19). At this moment, the Pharisees realized the people's allegiance would be either to Jesus' way or to their way, because, in their words, "the whole world has gone after him" (verse 19). Then Jesus gave a discourse predicting his impending death (see verses 20–36). The current was gaining speed as everything was rushing toward the waterfall of Calvary.

Journal:
- What do you think was going through the disciples' minds when Jesus told them that his hour had come?
- People responded in different ways to Jesus' life and teaching. Why do you think some believed and others rejected him?

Pray: Thank Jesus for setting his eyes and heart on Calvary and committing to pay the price for our sins. Ask for God to grow your faith bigger and deeper, even when there are clouds on the horizon and times look tough.

DAY 27

Read: John 13

Reflect: The pain of betrayal is deep and real—and it was even for Jesus. After washing his disciples' feet, he was troubled. He looked at the men gathered around the table and told them what was on his heart. One of them would betray him. They seemed shocked. We know what happened next, but what a soul-searching moment this must have been for each of the disciples. *Could Jesus be talking about me?* Think about what would have gone through your mind if you had been sitting there. Would you have instinctively pointed to Judas? Or allowed the light of the Holy Spirit shine on your heart and consider if betrayal was lurking in the dark corners of your own soul?

Journal:
- Why do you think Jesus was troubled and struggling with the reality that one of his disciples would betray him?
- If you had been at the table with Jesus, how might you have searched your own heart for seeds of betrayal?

Pray: Thank Jesus that he knows all the dark places in your heart and still loves you! Pray that you will grow in bold faith so that when temptation comes, you will stand strong in humble commitment to Jesus.

DAY 28

Memorize: Conclude this week's personal study by again reciting John 13:14–15:

> *"Now that I, your Lord and Teacher, have washed your feet, you also should wash one another's feet. I have set you an example that you should do as I have done for you."*

Reflect: Watch . . . learn . . . do! After Jesus reminded his disciples of who he was, he called them to do what they had just witnessed him doing. This simple process is how kids learn. How did you learn to have manners, tie a shoe, make a peanut and jelly sandwich, and everything else you know how to do? Someone gave you an example, then they explained how to do it, and finally they said, "Now you try it." The end result of Jesus' foot-washing ministry was to send all of his disciples (including us) into the world with a commitment to serve others. Have you heard the message? Do you get the point? Are you following your Savior's example?

TRUTH FOR THE CONFUSED

JOHN 14-16

*In tough times, the truth is still the truth. The problem
is, we forget what God has taught us and lose our
focus on what matters most. Jesus loves us and is
always ready to draw near and remind us of his truth.
When we are confused, he loves to bring clarity!*

WELCOME

The waves of trouble and confusion come crashing onto
the shores of every life. Someone might have given you the
impression that if you love Jesus and faithfully follow him, the
storms of life will always move north or south of you. Never-
ending blue skies will hover over you, financial resources will

magically appear in your checking account, relationships will be perpetually harmonious, and all your back pain will disappear. (You get the idea.)

Here's the problem. That theological worldview is simply untrue. In fact, it stands in direct opposition to the teaching of the Bible. A simple study of the lives of people who followed God's plan shows us that times of confusion, pain, and struggle were not the exception—*they were the norm.*

Consider Mary, the mother of Christ. She loved her family and walked in obedience to God, but she ultimately watched her firstborn son be tortured and crucified (see John 19:25).

The apostle Paul followed God's call and was devoted to sharing the good news of Jesus but he ended up with countless scars across his shoulders and back as a sign of his devotion to his Savior (see 2 Corinthians 11:24).

The disciple John served Jesus with all his heart, but he ended up imprisoned in a penal colony on the island of Patmos (see Revelation 1:9).

The question is not, "Will we face painful times that could test our faith?" Rather, it is, "Will we choose to believe in Jesus and hold to our faith in the middle of these challenging seasons?" In times of confusion, loss, and sorrow, Jesus reaches out and offers us the truth. He does not promise always to remove the pain, but his truth (and by the way, Jesus *is* Truth) will sustain us. Our Savior does not promise a trouble-free life, but he gives clarity in the confusion.

When we believe Jesus, take him at his word, and embrace his truth, we can press on in faith. We can stand strong—even when we don't totally understand what is happening or why we are facing the storms of this life.

SHARE

Tell about a time when you faced one of life's storms and how it opened the door to confusion, struggle, or even a crisis of faith. How did Jesus draw near, remind you of the truth, and help you make it through?

WATCH

Play the video for session five. As you watch, use the following outline to record any thoughts, questions, or key points that stand out to you.

The discourses of Jesus

Our ideas of what we need in times of trouble are quite different from Jesus' ideas.

In times of trouble and confusion, remember the hope of heaven (John 14:2–14).

In times of trouble and confusion, know that you are not alone (John 14:15–31).

In times of trouble and confusion, remain in Jesus and keep bearing fruit (John 15:1–17).

In times of trouble and confusion, remember who wins and has overcome (John 16:16–33).

In times of trouble and confusion, keep believing in Jesus.

DISCUSS

Take a few minutes to discuss with your group members what you just watched and to explore these concepts in Scripture. Use the following questions to help guide your discussion.

I. What impacted you the most as you watched Kyle's teaching on John 14–16?

2. **Read John 14:1.** What were some of the things that could have been troubling the hearts of the disciples at the moment Jesus spoke these words? Share one thing that is troubling your heart and mind today, and let your group members know how they can be praying for you.

3. **Read John 14:2–9.** What do you learn about the hope Jesus brings his followers in confusing times? How does the hope of heaven help you in times of struggle and ambiguity?

4. **Read John 14:15–20** and **John 14:25–27.** What does Jesus teach his followers about the Holy Spirit? How can this truth bring clarity in times of confusion? Tell about one way you have experienced the presence, power, and comfort of the Holy Spirit in a challenging time of life.

5. **Read John 15:1–9.** Right in the middle of a time of turmoil, Jesus told his disciples they were to abide (remain) in him. In light of this passage, what does it mean to abide in Jesus? What is one way you have tried to live out Jesus' call to stay closely connected to him no matter what you are facing?

6. **Read John 16:29–33.** Jesus finished this amazing discourse by assuring his followers that they should take heart because he has won the victory and overcome the world. In the midst of all they had faced and would face in the coming days (the trials, crucifixion, resurrection, and ascension of Jesus) how do you think these words helped them press on? How does the victory of Jesus bring you hope, courage, and focus, even in confusing times?

MEMORIZE

Your memory verse for this week is John 14:1:

> *"Do not let your hearts be troubled. You believe in God;*
> *believe also in me."*

Recite this verse out loud. Ask for volunteers who would like
to say the verse from memory.

RESPOND

What will you take away from this session? What is one practical next step you can take to hold to the truth Jesus taught
when you are going through confusing and difficult times?

PRAY

Close your group time by praying in any of these directions:

- Give thanks to God for giving us these powerful teachings of Jesus that give us truth to sustain us in this life.
- Lift up members of your group by praying for God's truth to strengthen them and bring hope as they walk through painful and challenging times.
- Pray for the Holy Spirit to bring the truth of Scripture to your heart and mind when life's storms are raging around you. Pray this for your group members as well.

SESSION FIVE

Reflect on the material you have covered in this session by engaging in the following between-session learning resources. Each week you will begin by reviewing the key verse(s) to memorize for the session. During the next six days, you will have an opportunity to read a portion of John's Gospel and reflect on what you learn, respond by taking action, journal some of your insights, and pray about what God has taught you. Finally, on the last day, you will review the key verse(s) and reflect on what you have learned for the week.

DAY 29

Memorize. Begin this week's personal study by reciting the following verse found in John 14:1:

"Do not let your hearts be troubled. You believe in God; believe also in me."

Now try to say the verse from memory.

Reflect: Think about the setting of these words. Jesus had just washed his disciples' feet and told them they were called by God to do the same for others. At the table where they shared the Last Supper, the Lord told them that one of their tight-knit group of twelve would betray him. They had heard Jesus tell Peter (the Rock!) that Peter would disown him three times before the rooster crowed. To top it all off, Jesus had told them that he was going away and they could not come with him. Then Jesus added, "Do not let your hearts be troubled." It becomes very clear very quickly that true belief in Jesus has power to overcome a lot of confusion.

DAY 30

Read: John 14

Reflect: In one of the boldest declarations in the history of the world, Jesus said, "I am the way and the truth and the life. No one comes to the Father except through me" (verse 6). In one sentence, Jesus drew a line, not in the sand, but in all eternity. "I am the way, the only way to heaven and a relationship with God the Father." What a massive claim! He said, "I am the truth." Not "a" truth but "the truth." These were the utterances of either a megalomaniac or God in human form. To cap it off, Jesus said, "I am the life." Through John's Gospel, we learn that Jesus meant *life* in virtually every way. He is the creator of life, the giver of life, the way to abundant life, and the pathway to eternal life.

Journal:

- If the early disciples believed each claim Jesus made in John 14:6, how should this have impacted their faith and lives?
- If you accept each of these declarations of Jesus as absolutely true, how should it impact the way you follow Jesus and live for him?

Pray: Spend time in prayer declaring your confidence that Jesus is the Way, Truth, and Life. Commit to follow his ways, embrace his truth, and share his life with others.

DAY 31

Read: John 15

Reflect: I am a friend of God. That sounds almost arrogant, and it would be if it were not absolutely true (see verses 14–15). When a follower of Jesus declares they are a friend of the Savior, God with us, they are simply agreeing with the truth Jesus stated.

There is an intimacy to the very idea that can feel too familiar and comfortable. But we should get used to it. Our Lord spoke truth into our confusion. We can see ourselves as unloved, left out, and insignificant. The world and the forces of hell love to reinforce these lies. Jesus tells us who we are. Have you come to the cross and received the free gift of grace? Have you taken the hand of the Savior? Are you seeking to follow his lead? Then you are a friend of God—get used to it!

Journal:
- What are some of the reasons we might be uncomfortable seeing ourselves as loved and valued friends of God?
- If you embrace the truth that you are a friend of God, how could this impact the way you see yourself and other followers of Jesus?

Pray: Thank Jesus that he sees you as his friend. Pray for a growing intimacy with Jesus as you delight in the friendship you have with him.

DAY 32

Read: John 16

Reflect: Loneliness is an epidemic in our world. Here's the good news: once a person places faith in Jesus, they are never alone. The Spirit of the living God, the Comforter, the Advocate, comes and dwells in us. What an amazing truth! What a source of hope and encouragement! Jesus went so far as to say that it was better for his disciples that he would go away because the Spirit of Truth would come to them and never leave (see verse 7). At that moment, this news would have sounded confusing to them. What could be better than having Jesus right there with them? But they discovered what we have also learned. When the Holy Spirit moves in, he leads, teaches, convicts, gifts, grows fruit, empowers, comforts, and so much more.

Journal:
- What does the Bible promise us about the Holy Spirit?
- How have you experienced these truths, and how is the Holy Spirit at work in your life right now?

Pray: Thank Jesus for sending the Holy Spirit to be in you and to guide you. Pray for a humble heart that is responsive to the leading and conviction of the Holy Spirit.

DAY 33

Read: John 17

Reflect: Most people refer to the prayer of Jesus found in the Sermon on the Mount (see Matthew 6:9–13) as the "Lord's Prayer," and that's fine. But in a very real sense, that brief prayer might better be called "The Disciples' Prayer." If you remember, the disciples had come to Jesus and asked him to teach them to pray. It was a didactic moment when Jesus was giving them a model to use as they talked with their heavenly Father. What we find here in John 17 is Jesus' longest recorded prayer. He was not responding to a request to teach others to pray. Prayer was erupting from deep within our Savior's heart. The entire chapter is our Lord talking to the Father. Read slowly, and picture Jesus looking up to heaven and lifting these words as a prayer for himself, for his followers (including you), and for the world!

Journal:
- What things was Jesus moved to pray for in this chapter?
- What can you learn about prayer as you listen to the heart of Jesus in John 17?

Pray: Read this chapter as a prayer from the heart of Jesus, and join in with him as you feel led.

DAY 34

Read: John 18

Reflect: Moving to this chapter in John can give you whiplash! One moment, Jesus and his disciples are in a pastoral setting, as Jesus prays to the Father. Then Jesus moves with his followers across the Kidron Valley and into a garden. This would not be a peaceful place! A mob comes looking for Jesus, led by one of his closest followers, Judas. Words are exchanged. Swords are drawn. Blood is spilled. Jesus is arrested and bound. Peter denies that he even knows Jesus. The sinless Lamb of God is rushed through a series of mock trials. The governor asks the mob that has gathered if they want him to release Jesus, and they scream, "Give us Barabbas!" Things have changed dramatically!

Journal:
- As you read John 18, what battles and conflicts do you see coming to the surface?
- How did Jesus respond to the conflict, betrayal, and lies?

Pray: Thank Jesus for making the decision to go to the cross and die for your sins. Confess your continued need for the grace that he gives so freely.

DAY 35

Memorize: Conclude this week's personal study by again reciting John 14:1:

"Do not let your hearts be troubled. You believe in God; believe also in me."

Reflect: All through the Gospels, Jesus made it crystal clear that he was divine. He was God with us. Notice his words in this passage. He reminded his disciples that they "believe in God." Then he called them to "believe also in me." There seems to be a one-to-one connection here. As you believe in God, so believe in me. Why could Jesus say this? Because he was fully divine. He and the Father were one. If they had seen him, they had seen the Father. Jesus would go on to reaffirm this over and over in the rest of the discourse (see John 14–16). Hold to this truth in good times and in confusing times: Jesus is God!

WE HAVE SEEN HIS GLORY

JOHN 20

Belief in Jesus can be challenging. Even after the Savior rose from the dead and many of the disciples declared they had seen him, Thomas struggled with doubt. But to be honest, all of us can have our moments of wondering and dealing with doubt. The question is not whether we will have moments of uncertainty but how we will deal with doubts when they come.

WELCOME

We live in a time of growing doubt. The days of people blindly trusting those in authority are long gone. Each passing decade leads to increased erosion of trust in almost every area of life.

Not too long ago, evening news anchors were ranked as some of the most trusted people in our society. Viewers would tune in every night and take what they heard as accurate, balanced, and objective reporting. There was a built-in confidence that each word in a newscast had authority and could be believed. Now there is an ever-increasing shadow of doubt when it comes to declarations made by news personalities.

Doctors, nurses, and medical professionals were once seen as honest people who chose their vocations with altruistic motives. They were trusted at a high level, and people believed what they said. Now skepticism has become much more common and people want a second or third opinion before trusting what their medical professional says. Trust is on the decline.

Law enforcement professionals used to be celebrated. Scientists were seen as experts in their fields. Pastors and priests were seen as protectors of truth and examples of moral trustworthiness. School teachers were trained to educate children, and few worried about ulterior motives or agendas.

You get the picture. Those days are growing smaller and smaller in the rearview mirror of history.

With the rapid disintegration of trust in almost every area of life, is it surprising that so many people are questioning their faith? Wondering if what they have always believed is really true? Even scrutinizing the ideas taught in God's Word? Should we be surprised that people today are dealing with doubt on a deep and personal level?

SHARE

Talk about an area where you have seen people's belief and trust erode and doubt creep in that has impacted their lives—and perhaps even their faith.

WATCH

Play the video for session six. As you watch, use the following outline to record any thoughts, questions, or key points that stand out to you.

Thomas faced the two big questions we all will face: What do I really believe? What do I believe about Jesus?

Thomas missed the first time Jesus appeared to the disciples (John 20:19–23).

Thomas expressed his struggles and doubts (John 20:24–25).

Thomas was there the second time Jesus came to the disciples, and he affirmed his belief in Jesus (John 20:26–29).

Three things that helped Thomas move from being an uncertain doubter to a confident believer:

1. He wanted to believe and was honest about his doubts.

2. He intentionally put himself in an environment where he could discover truth.

3. He was willing to look at the evidence.

Stories of skeptics becoming devoted followers of Jesus:

An invitation to face doubts, ask questions, and encounter Jesus:

DISCUSS

Take a few minutes to discuss with your group members what you just watched and to explore these concepts in Scripture. Use the following questions to help guide your discussion.

I. What impacted you the most as you watched Kyle's teaching on John 20?

2. **Read John 20:19–23.** What did Jesus say and do that would have strengthened the disciples' faith and confidence in him? What did Thomas miss?

3. **Read John 20:24–25.** Why do you think Thomas responded the way he did to the testimony of the other disciples? What did Thomas say he needed in order to reestablish his foundations of belief in Jesus?

4. **Read John 20:26–29.** How did Jesus meet Thomas right where he was, and what did this do for Thomas's faith and confidence in Jesus? Tell about a time Jesus met you right where you were and how this fortified your belief in him.

5. Thomas did three distinct things that helped him move from doubt to belief. How can each of these help a person move from doubting to a more confident faith?

- ○ Wanting to believe but being truly honest about your doubts about faith
- ○ Putting yourself in a place and mindset where you can discover the truth about Jesus
- ○ Being curious and willing to look at the evidence for Jesus

6. Tell a story about someone who went from doubting and questioning faith to becoming a devoted and authentic follower of Jesus. How do stories like this inspire you and deepen your faith?

MEMORIZE

Your memory verse for this final week is John 20:28:

Thomas said to him, "My Lord and my God!"

Recite this verse out loud. Ask for volunteers who would like to say the verse from memory.

RESPOND

What will you take away from this session? What is one practical next step you can take that will help you face and overcome doubt as you increase your belief in Jesus?

PRAY

Close your group time by praying in any of these directions:

- Ask for courage to be honest and admit any area in which you are struggling with doubts and questions about your faith.
- Thank Jesus for ways he has met you right where you are and led you closer to the heart of the Father.
- Pray for a person in your life who does not know Jesus. Ask God to meet them where they are, reveal his presence and grace, and draw them to the heart of Jesus.

SESSION SIX

Reflect on the material you have covered in this session by engaging in the following between-session learning resources. Each week you will begin by reviewing the key verse(s) to memorize for the session. During the next six days, you will have an opportunity to read a portion of John's Gospel and reflect on what you learn, respond by taking action, journal some of your insights, and pray about what God has taught you. Finally, on the last day, you will review the key verse(s) and reflect on what you have learned for the week.

DAY 36

Memorize: Begin this week's personal study by reciting the following verse found in John 20:28:

Thomas said to him, "My Lord and my God"

Now try to say the verse from memory.

Reflect: When Thomas called Jesus "my Lord and my God," he was speaking words of surrender to the leadership of Jesus in his life. When he recognized that Jesus was alive and had conquered sin, Satan, death, and hell, he surrendered to the absolute authority of Jesus. This week, think about ways that you can surrender to the leadership of the risen Savior in any areas of your life where you are holding back.

DAY 37

Read: John 19

Reflect: Jesus was sentenced, crucified, and placed in a tomb. If you were playing tennis, you would say, "Game, set, match!" But if you are a Christian, you know that even death was not the end of Jesus' story. From a human standpoint, the end of John's 19 is the final nail in the coffin. The story is over. Hope is dead. Jesus lost. But there are still two more chapters! Even death is not the end when it comes to Jesus.

Journal:
- If you were one of the disciples, how might you have felt at the end of John 19?
- If John 19 was the end of the Gospel and the end of Jesus' story, what would that have meant for the followers of Jesus in the first century and today?

Pray: Thank Jesus today for choosing to take the nails, bear your shame, and die in your place.

DAY 38

Read: John 20

Reflect: Putting all the pieces together was a challenge. Mary was shocked that the tomb was empty, but she was still looking for a body (see verse 2). Peter and John had a footrace to the tomb, and when they saw that Jesus' body was gone, "they still did not understand from Scripture that Jesus had to rise from the dead" (verse 9). The first time Jesus appeared to the disciples in a locked room, he showed his pierced hands and side to help them grasp that he was now alive (see verse 20). When the disciples assured Thomas that they had seen the Lord, the struggling disciple said that he would not believe until he could "put my hand into his side" (verse 25). There was plenty of doubt to go around! We heap most of it on Thomas, but the truth is that he was in good company.

Journal:
- What are some ways the early disciples struggled with questions and doubts about the resurrection of Jesus?
- What are ways Christians today struggle with doubts about Jesus? What can we do to decrease our doubts?

Pray: Thank Jesus for his resurrection, for his appearances, and for how he shows up and reveals his presence in your life.

DAY 39

Read: John 21

Reflect: Peter must have felt defeated. He was sure he would never let Jesus down or deny his Lord in any way. Peter was a man of conviction and confidence. Yet when the pressure was on, he denied his Lord three times. When he realized what he had done, he "wept bitterly" (Luke 22:62). Now Jesus was alive and talking face-to-face with him. What grace. What healing. What restoration (see John 21:15–19). As Peter is drowning in guilt and sorrow, Jesus throws him a lifeline. Our restoring Savior spoke the same words to Peter that he had uttered three years earlier, "Follow me" (Matthew 4:19; John 21:19).

Journal:
- What are ways the enemy tries to get you to dwell on past failures so you feel you are not worthy to serve God?
- Why is it important for you to hear Jesus say, "Follow me," both today and every day?

Pray: Thank Jesus for lavishing you with grace, new beginnings, and invitations to follow him. Pray for courage to get up and follow Jesus again and again and again!

DAY 40

Memorize: Conclude your forty-day personal study by again reciting this verse found in John 20:28:

Thomas said to him, "My Lord and my God!"

Now try to say this verse completely from memory.

Reflect: Not only did Thomas declare Jesus the Lord (Leader) of his life, but he made a profound theological affirmation. Thomas said, "Jesus, you are my God!" This is truly amazing! Just a week earlier Thomas was in a doubting frame of mind. Now he was ready to fall on his face and worship Jesus as the divine incarnate God. The resurrection, when we understand what it means, assures us that Jesus was and is God with us. We should follow him as Lord and worship him as our God. What is one way you can worship Jesus with fresh passion and devotion?

LEADER'S GUIDE

Thank you for your willingness to lead your group through this study! What you have chosen to do is valuable and will make a great difference in the lives of others. The rewards of being a leader are different from those of participating, and we hope that as you lead you will find your own walk with Jesus deepened by this experience.

This study on the Gospel of John in the *40 Days Through the Book* series is built around video content and small-group interaction. As the group leader, think of yourself as the host. Your job is to take care of your guests by managing the behind-the-scenes details so that when everyone arrives, they can enjoy their time together. As the leader, your role is not to answer all the questions or reteach the content—the video and study guide will do that work. Your role is to guide the experience and cultivate your group into a teaching community. This will make it a place for members to process, question, and reflect on the teaching.

Before your first meeting, make sure everyone has a copy of the study guide. This will keep everyone on the same page and help the process run more smoothly. If members are unable to purchase the guide, arrange it so they can share with other members. Giving everyone access to the material will position this study to be as rewarding as possible. Everyone should feel free to write in his or her study guide and bring it to group every week.

SETTING UP THE GROUP

Your group will need to determine how long you want to meet each week so you can plan your time accordingly. Generally, most groups like to meet for either sixty minutes or ninety minutes, so you could use one of the following schedules:

SECTION	60 MINUTES	90 MINUTES
WELCOME (members arrive and get settled)	5 minutes	5 minutes
SHARE (discuss one of the opening questions for the session)	5 minutes	10 minutes
READ (discuss the questions based on the Scripture reading for the session)	5 minutes	10 minutes
WATCH (watch the video teaching material together and take notes)	15 minutes	15 minutes
DISCUSS (discuss the Bible study questions based on the video teaching)	25 minutes	40 minutes
RESPOND/PRAY (reflect on the key insights, pray together, and dismiss)	5 minutes	10 minutes

As the group leader, you will want to create an environment that encourages sharing and learning. A church sanctuary or formal classroom may not be as ideal as a living room, because those locations can feel formal and less intimate. No matter what setting you choose, provide enough comfortable seating for everyone, and, if possible, arrange the seats in a semicircle so everyone can see the video easily. This will make the transition between the video and group conversation more efficient and natural.

Also, try to get to the meeting site early so you can greet participants as they arrive. Simple refreshments create a welcoming atmosphere and can be a wonderful addition to a group study. Try to take food and pet allergies into account to make your guests as comfortable as possible. You may also want to consider offering childcare to couples with children who want to attend. Finally, be sure your media technology is working properly. Managing these details up front will make the rest of your group experience flow smoothly and provide a welcoming space in which to engage the content of this study on the Gospel of John.

STARTING THE GROUP TIME

Once everyone has arrived, it is time to begin the study. Here are some simple tips to make your group time healthy, enjoyable, and effective.

Begin the meeting with a short prayer and remind the group members to put their phones on silent. This is a way to make sure you can all be present with one another and with God. Next, give each person a few minutes to respond to the questions in the "Share" section. This won't require as much time in session one, but beginning in session two, people may need more time to share their insights from their personal studies. Usually, you won't answer the discussion questions yourself, but you should go first with the "Share" questions, answering briefly and with a reasonable amount of transparency.

At the end of session one, invite the group members to complete the "Your 40-Day Journey" for that week. Explain that they can share any insights the following week before the video teaching. Let them know it's not a problem if they can't get to these activities some weeks. It will still be beneficial for them to hear from the other participants in the group.

LEADING THE DISCUSSION TIME

Now that the group is engaged, watch the video and respond with some directed small-group discussion. Encourage the group members to participate in the discussion, but make sure they know this is not mandatory for the group, so as to not make them feel pressured to come up with an answer. As the discussion progresses, follow up with comments such as, "Tell me more about that," or, "Why did you answer that way?" This will allow the group participants to deepen their reflections and invite a meaningful conversation in a nonthreatening way.

Note that you have been given multiple questions to use in each session, and you do not have to use them all or even follow them in order. Feel free to pick and choose questions based on the needs of your group or how the conversation is flowing. Also, don't be afraid of silence. Offering a question and allowing up to thirty seconds of silence is okay. This space allows people to think about how they want to respond and gives them time to do so.

As group leader, you are the boundary keeper for your group. Do not let anyone (yourself included) dominate the group time. Keep an eye out for group members who might be tempted to "attack" folks they disagree with or try to "fix" those having struggles. These kinds of behaviors can derail a group's momentum, so they need to be steered in a different direction. Model active listening and encourage everyone in your group to do the same. This will make your group time a safe space and create a positive community.

The group discussion leads to a closing time of individual reflection and prayer. Encourage the participants to review what they have learned and write down their thoughts to the "Respond" section. Close by taking a few minutes to pray as directed as a group.

Thank you again for taking the time to lead your group. You are making a difference in the lives of others and having an impact on the kingdom of God!

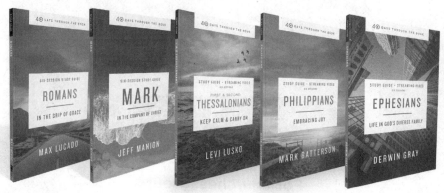

MORE FROM
KYLE IDLEMAN

Trade Book

ON SALE JUNE 2023

Bible Study Guide + Streaming Video
(DVD also available)

ON SALE JUNE 2023

AVAILABLE WHEREVER BOOKS ARE SOLD.

New Testament
Everyday Bible Study Series

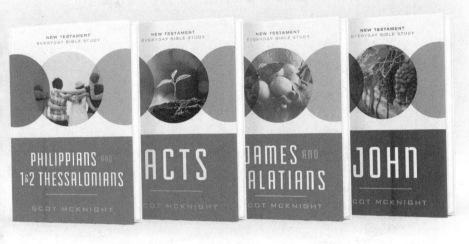

In the **New Testament Everyday Bible Study Series**, widely respected biblical scholar Scot McKnight combines interpretive insights with pastoral wisdom for all the books of the New Testament.

Each volume provides:

- Original Meaning. Brief, precise expositions of the biblical text and offers a clear focus for the central message of each passage.

- Fresh Interpretation. Brings the passage alive with fresh images and what it means to follow King Jesus.

- Practical Application. Biblical connections and questions for reflection and application for each passage.

— AVAILABLE IN THE SERIES —

James and Galatians

Acts

Philippians and 1 & 2 Thessalonians

John

The Jesus Bible Study Series

Beginnings
ISBN 9780310154983
On sale January 2023

People
ISBN 9780310155027
On sale September 2023

Church
ISBN 9780310155065
On sale April 2024

Revolt
ISBN 9780310155003
On sale April 2023

Savior
ISBN 9780310155041
On sale January 2024

Forever
ISBN 9780310155089
On sale September 2024

Available wherever books are sold

Harper*Christian* Resources

passionpublishing